NEW BOOKS FOR NEW READERS

Judy Cheatham
General Editor

Why Work?

Judi Jennings

THE UNIVERSITY PRESS OF KENTUCKY

The New Books for New Readers project was made possible
through funding from the National Endowment for the Humanities,
the Kentucky Humanities Council, and *The Kentucky Post*.
The opinions and views expressed in this book are not necessarily
those of the Kentucky Humanities Council.

Maps by Alan Clinkinbeard.

Published by The University Press of Kentucky
Scholarly publisher for the Commonwealth,
serving Bellarmine College, Berea College, Centre
College of Kentucky, Eastern Kentucky University,
The Filson Club, Georgetown College, Kentucky
Historical Society, Kentucky State University,
Morehead State University, Murray State University,
Northern Kentucky University, Transylvania University,
University of Kentucky, University of Louisville,
and Western Kentucky University.
Editorial and Sales Offices: Lexington, Kentucky 40506-0336

Library of Congress Cataloging-in-Publication Data

Jennings, Judi, 1947-
    Why work? / Judi Jennings.
        p.   cm.—(New books for new readers)
    ISBN 0-8131-0904-3
    1. Work.   2. Work—History.
I. Title.   II. Series.
HD4901.J46   1989
306.36—dc20   89-38086

Contents

This work is dedicated to the members of the Pike County Adult Reading Program who helped write it: Bobbi Bridgeman, Christine Bridgeman, Bruce Cantrell, Kathy Cantrell, Frank Carlton, Veronica Click, Suzy Elliot, Sydney England, Aggie Fink, James Fink, Edith Freebody, Lula Gross, Edna Redwine, Sue Sexton, Shirley West, and Alice Yarus.

Foreword

The New Books for New Readers project was made possible through funding from the National Endowment for the Humanities, the Kentucky Humanities Council, and *The Kentucky Post*. The co-sponsorship and continuing assistance of the Kentucky Department for Libraries and Archives and the Kentucky Literacy Commission have been essential to our undertaking. We are also grateful for the advice and support provided to us by the University Press of Kentucky. All these agencies share our commitment to the important role that reading books should play in the lives of the people of our state, and their belief in this project has made it possible.

The Kentucky Humanities Council recognizes in the campaign for adult literacy a cause closely linked to our own mission, to make the rich heritage of the humanities accessible to all Kentuckians. Because the printed word is a vital source of this heritage, we believe that books focused on our state's history and culture and written for adults who are newly learning to read can help us to serve a group of Kentucky's citizens not always reached or served by our programs. We offer these books in the hope that they will be of value to adult new readers in their quest, through words, for an understanding of what it means to be human.

Ramona Lumpkin, Executive Director
Kentucky Humanities Council

Acknowledgments

This book has been produced with support from the National Endowment for the Humanities, the Kentucky Humanities Council, the Kentucky Literacy Commission, and the University Press of Kentucky. I would like to express special appreciation to Bruce Cantrell, Susan Sexton, and Aggie Fink. Many thanks go to Aggie Fink for her comments and suggestions. The book would not have been possible without the friendship and cooperation of Sydney England and other tutors in the Pike County Adult Reading Program. Judy Cheatham was patient, helpful, and understanding. She was generous with her time, her suggestions, and her support.

How Does It Work?

What do you think of when you read the word *work*? Many things could come to mind. *Work* can be a place, as in "Where do you work?" *Work* can be a job, as in "What is your work?" *Work* can be a thing, as in "This is a great piece of work." *Work* can be an action, as in "How does this computer work?"

People get worked up. Mines get worked out. Students work problems. Knitters work patterns. Farmers work land. Many people are overworked, but things usually work out. We have earthworks, fireworks, and artworks. And sometimes you get a really good hamburger with all the works.

The word *work* has taken on many meanings. Can you think of others? Is work something you think about much? If so, you are not alone. Work is an important part of human life; it has many different forms and meanings.

Whether or not you work for pay and when and how you work determine a great deal about how you live. For example, when you go to sleep and when you wake up could depend on your hours of work. Work determines where many people live. More and more men and women today move from one place to another to keep a job or to find a better one. But others stay in one place and look for work there. If you had to choose, would you move or would you stay?

Some people get paid more for their work than others. Sometimes people say that those who get paid more are "worth" more than those who are paid less. Do you think a person's worth is determined by how much he or she is paid? Of course, those who make more money can buy more clothes, cars, and other things. Do you think money makes people worth more?

What about people who do not or cannot work for pay? Sometimes when elderly people retire, they say they feel useless or worthless. When people are unemployed and cannot find a good job, they may also feel worthless. Since women do not get paid for cooking, cleaning, or caring for children in their own homes, some people do not consider those things work. What do you think?

Work has been part of human history from the beginning and even before. Since work plays a big part in all our lives, it is important to understand as much about it as we can. One way to do that is to look at the history of work. How has work changed over hundreds of years? How did people in other times and places work? How have new machines and new ideas changed the way we work and what we think about work?

Work Like Your Life Depended on It

In the first chapter you read that work was an important part of human life even before the beginning of history. How can that be? And how do we know what happened before the beginning of history, anyway?

Much about the beginning of human life on this earth is a mystery. We have signs that humans have been around for more than 125 thousand years. For many thousands of years, no humans knew how to read or write. Can you imagine living in a world where no one could read or write?

History is the study of the writings of the past. So the study of history begins when men and women learned to read and write. The time before reading and writing were invented is called *pre*history, or before history.

If prehistoric men and women could not read and write, then how do we know about work in prehistoric times? Many experts are trying to figure what life was like before people could read and write. These experts look for tools, weapons, bones, pottery, and anything else they can find. They study these things to find out how people lived.

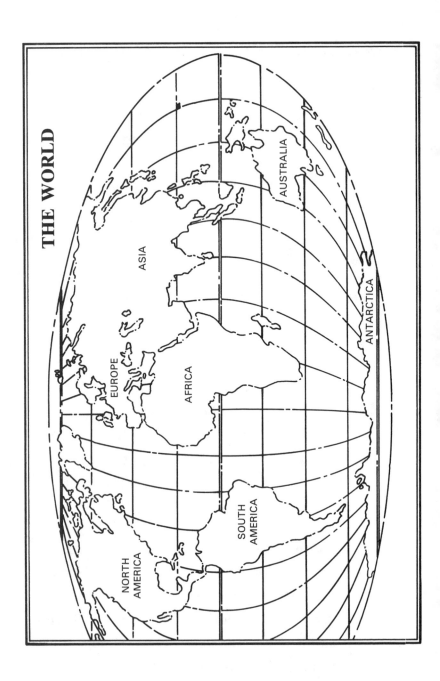

THE WORLD

NORTH AMERICA

SOUTH AMERICA

EUROPE

AFRICA

ASIA

AUSTRALIA

ANTARCTICA

Thousands of years ago, people had to work to stay alive. Take Native Americans, for example. Today, the United States is part of North America. Can you find North America on the map of the world? In prehistoric times, North America was filled with many different groups of Native American people. Native American groups spoke different languages and lived different ways.

But they all had to work. They did not work for pay because there was no money. They had to work to get the things they needed to live. So even though they made no money, we could say they worked for their living.

About 12 thousand years ago, prehistoric people hunted large animals for food. From bones that have been found, we know that some of these animals were as big as elephants. And people then didn't have guns or metal knives. They had to make weapons. They chipped stones to make points for spears. Can you imagine hunting an elephant with a stone spear?

Hunting was one kind of work, but people did other kinds of work, too. Women gathered wild plants and berries, prepared food to eat, made clothes by sewing skins and furs, and took care of children and sick people. Men cleared the land, built shelters, and fought dangerous animals—and dangerous people, too. But prehistoric people probably didn't work as many hours each day as we do now. After all, they did not earn extra money for overtime!

About seven thousand to ten thousand years ago, many big animals started dying out. Then the Native people in North America had to figure out new ways to get food. The men hunted smaller animals, like deer, elk, raccoon, and opossum. Men learned to fish and catch birds. Women learned to grow corn, gourds, squash, and peppers for food. And they didn't have any labor-saving devices like tractors and tillers!

After prehistoric people started growing their own food, they figured out how to do many other things. Women made baskets and pots. Men learned to irrigate the land. Different groups figured out how to do different things at different times. The Maya people who lived in what is today Mexico and Central America drew picture words they could read.

Most prehistoric people in North America never learned to read and write. But they could do many other things. They had to remember everything they needed to know. They probably told each other stories to help them remember. And they drew pictures. Have you ever used these ways of remembering things?

In some ways, people in prehistoric times were different than we are today. But in some ways they were the same. People had to work, although they did not get paid money for it. Not all work was the same, and people did different things. Hunting, fishing, and growing plants were work for them. Would you have liked to have worked for a living back then?

Keeping At It Gets the Work Done

As you know, prehistoric people tried to figure out new ways of doing things. People today still seem to be trying to come up with new ways to do work quicker and better. Do you like to figure out new ways to do things?

Like Native Americans, different groups of people in other parts of the world figured out how to do things at different times. About three thousand years ago, people living in Greece (called Greeks) began to figure out how to read and write. Find Greece on the map. What countries is it near? What sea is it near? Today Greece is one country, but long ago Greece was made up of many separate cities.

Like the North Americans in prehistoric times, at first Greeks did not know how to read and write. So, like prehistoric people, the Greeks made up songs and poems to help them remember. When the Greeks learned to write, they wrote down some of their songs and poems.

One of the first Greeks to write down poems was a man named Hesiod. More than two thousand years ago, he wrote a long poem called "Works and Days. " We can learn a lot about work in those days from his poem.

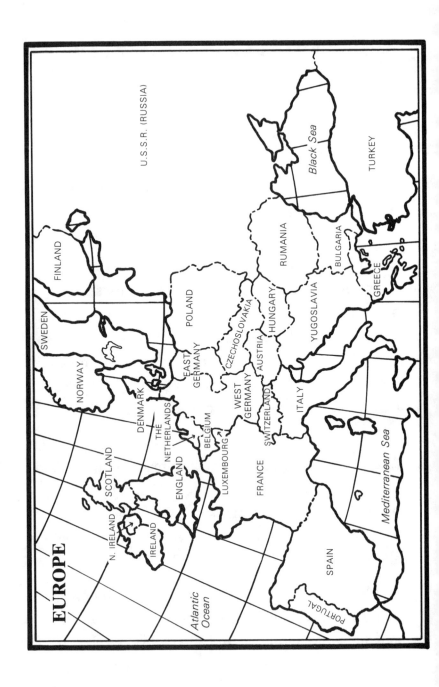

EUROPE

24

Work was important to Hesiod. The kind of work he wrote most about was farming. In Hesiod's time, farmers in Greece grew wheat to make bread and grapes to make wine. They also kept sheep for wool and goats for milk and cheese. They used oxen for plowing.

Hesiod had lots of advice for farmers. He advised farmers to plow in October "when you hear the cry of the crane going over." Farmers should prune the grapevines before "the swallow calls" in April. Farmers must be ready to work hard "when snails crawl" in May. Do you know farmers today who go by signs like this?

Hesiod mentioned other kind of work. He wrote about potters, carpenters, and blacksmiths. "It is best to work at whatever you have a talent for doing," he wrote. But he thought trading by sea was dangerous and should be avoided.

Hesiod believed it was important to work hard. "Work is no disgrace," he wrote. "The disgrace is in not working. . . . Don't put off work another day, or even until tomorrow," he advised. "It is keeping at it that gets the work done." Do you hear people say things like that today?

Hesiod said, "A man looks at his neighbor, who is rich, then he, too, wants work; for the rich man presses on with his plowing and planting. So the neighbor envies the neighbor, who presses on toward wealth." Do you think people work hard so they will be wealthy? Do you think people envy wealthy people and want to be like them?

Hesiod was a free man who owned land. Like all of us, he saw things from his own point of view. At that time, many Greeks made slaves of people from other places. These slaves had to do a lot of hard work. Hesiod gave advice about what work slaves should do.

Hesiod thought being poor was a shame. He said poor men were humble, while the rich were self-assured. He said being poor was "hateful" and "heart-eating." Do you think being poor is something to be ashamed of? Do you think Hesiod might have felt different if he had been a slave or a poor man?

Hesiod did not trust women. He wrote, "Don't let a woman, wiggling her behind, and flattering and coaxing take you in. . . . . Woman is just a cheat," said Hesiod. He thought a husband must teach his wife good manners. He thought a wife should stay at home and spin and weave. Do you think a Greek woman of that time might have had a different point of view?

After Hesiod, other Greeks wrote about many

other things. They wrote about history, plays, and ideas. They studied medicine, built beautiful buildings, and played sports. They had money and used banks. They wrote down laws and figured out a new system of government run by free men like Hesiod. They called their government democracy.

After the Greeks learned to read and write, they could do many things they couldn't do before. Can you think of other things people can do when they can read and write?

Work in the City of Ladies

As you know from reading the last chapter, the Greeks figured out how to do many fine things a long time ago. But the Greeks weren't perfect. Greeks living in different cities fussed and fought with each other. A little more than two thousand years ago, the Greek cities were taken over by another big city. That city was Rome, in what is now Italy. Can you find Italy on a map? Now, look for Rome.

The Romans liked many of the Greek ways of doing things. The Romans copied many Greek artworks and ideas. The Romans also invented some new things of their own, like a government that was a republic and had a senate. The Romans were good soldiers; they knew how to fight. They fought people all around them and ruled many lands.

For a long time, the Romans had a great empire. But some people didn't like being ruled by Rome and fought against Rome every chance they got. Finally, about 15 hundred years ago, people outside Rome defeated the army and took over the city!

Today, we call the one thousand or so years after the defeat of Rome the Middle Ages. We call those years the *Middle* Ages because they came *after* the fall of Rome but *before* modern times. They were in the middle. Of course, people back then did not say they were living in the Middle Ages. How could they know what was coming after them?

After the defeat of Rome, people had to figure out new ways of doing almost everything. The old ways of the Greeks and Romans were almost forgotten. But not everyone could agree on which new ways were the best. So they fussed and fought some more.

With all the fighting going on in the Middle Ages, land became very important. People needed land for food, so whoever owned land had power. After a while, the man who owned the most land became the king. A few women had land and power, but not many. Other men who owned a lot of land became nobles. Usually, a woman was a noble only if her father or husband was one.

There was not enough land for everyone. Some people had little plots of land. Others had none. A man's status was based on how much land he owned. But a woman's status was almost always based on a man's—either her father or her husband. Status was important in the Middle Ages. Do you think status is important today? Is a man's status still based on his land? Is a woman's status still based on her man's?

Christine de Pisan was a woman during the

Middle Ages who was able to make a living on her own. Christine was born in Italy. She moved to Paris, France, when she was a little girl. Can you find France on the map? Christine married at age 15 and had three children. Her husband died when she was 25, and she was left to support herself and her family.

First, Christine decided to get more education. Then, she began to write books. In 1405, she wrote *The Treasure of the City of Ladies*. Christine gave the books she wrote to rich and powerful people. They gave her gifts and money for her books. So she was able to earn her living by writing.

In *The Treasure of the City of Ladies*, Christine wrote about the kind of work women did in her time. She wrote about women of every status, but mostly about "great queens, ladies and princesses."

Christine described how a queen should spend her day. The queen should "rise quite early" and pray, then go to church and give money to the poor. She should help with government and dine with people of high status. After lunch, the queen should rest, sew, or do some other handiwork. Then she should go to church again, take a stroll, eat supper, say her prayers, and go to bed.

Christine thought a queen should help her husband

in every way. With all the fighting going on, Christine thought the queen should "be the means of peace." What if another "prince wished to make war against her husband, or if her husband wished to make war"? The queen should "do whatever she can to find a way to peace."

Christine also wrote about noble women. Unlike the queen, a noble woman "ought to know how to use weapons." She should have "the heart of a man." A noblewoman should "know how much her annual income is," "how much the revenue from her land is worth," and "all about work on the land." Then, Christine said, if the noblewoman "is left a widow, she will not be found ignorant."

Because Christine lived in the city, she knew more about queens and noblewomen than she knew about women on farms. Farm women "work very hard," she wrote, and "are commonly raised on black bread, salt pork, with only water to drink." She warned farm women not to allow their children "to steal grapes from someone else's garden at night (or in the daytime either)."

Like Hesiod in Greek times, Christine de Pisan wrote from her own point of view. Do you think status had anything to do with her point of view? Do you think being a woman had anything to do with her point of view? What is your point of view about women's work in the Middle Ages? What about women's work now?

Do You Want to Trade?

One kind of work you haven't read much about yet is trade. Trading is very important in the world today. People trade guns, knives, cars, stocks, bonds, and bad things like drugs. Little kids trade baseball cards, and big managers trade baseball players. Old-timers trade tales. Do you ever trade things?

Prehistoric people probably traded food, furs, stories, and other things. You may recall from your earlier reading that Hesiod wrote about trade in his time. Hesiod thought that trade by "stormy seagoing" was risky.

Trade almost disappeared with all the fighting after the defeat of Rome. But by the time Christine de Pisan was writing, around 1400, men and women were trading again. Christine wrote about traders in Italy, where she was born. She said traders there "go abroad, buy in large quantities, have a big turnover," send their goods "to every land in great bundles" and "earn enormous wealth."

In the Middle Ages, some men and women in Italy, France, and other places stayed home and made things to trade. Men made gold jewelry, armor,

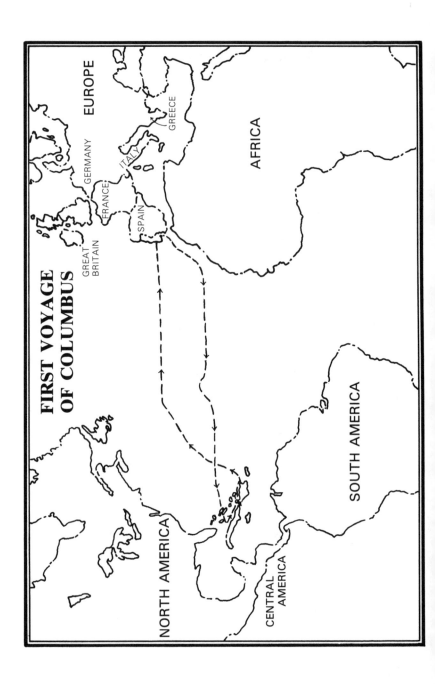

FIRST VOYAGE
OF COLUMBUS

EUROPE

GREAT
BRITAIN

GERMANY

FRANCE

ITALY

GREECE

SPAIN

AFRICA

NORTH AMERICA

CENTRAL
AMERICA

SOUTH AMERICA

bricks, and shoes. Women made silk cloth, girdles, and pancakes. Then, these men and women traded or sold the things they had made. Men and women who made things to trade became known as *trades*men and *trades*women. Their work was their *trade*. Do you hear people talk about a *trade* when they mean a kind of work?

Not long after the time of Christine de Pisan, trade got a big boost from Christopher Columbus. The "trade winds" carried the boats of Columbus and his men from Spain across the Atlantic. Columbus was surprised to find lands off the coast of North America. He thought he was in the Indies, so he called the people he saw "Indians." Columbus went back to Spain and told the people what he had found.

Columbus himself crossed the ocean several more times and others came after him. In the 1500s explorers went to Central and South America in search of gold and other things to trade. But the natives did not like more people coming to their land (and they didn't like being called Indians, either), so fighting broke out. The natives lost.

In the 1600s and 1700s, people crossed the Atlantic from France, Britain, and other countries. These people went to North America in search of things to trade. The natives of North America didn't like people coming to their land any better than the natives of Central and South America had. And they didn't like being called Indians, either. There was lots of fighting. The natives lost again.

Trade was important to the people who came to North America. People traded things they grew or got, like tobacco and furs. They traded for things they wanted from home. One of the things they wanted was wool cloth. There wasn't much else to make clothes with in those days.

Joseph Woods was a man who sold wool cloth in London, England, in the 1700s. Joseph bought wool cloth in northern England. He sold some of it in London and sent some of it to the American lands. Joseph said what he did most was "buying, selling, dining, reading, sleeping and smoking." How many of those things do you like to do?

But Joseph Woods did more than he said. He was married to the daughter of a rich banker. They had four children, three boys and one girl. Joseph had his wool shop and a sleeping room in the City of London. His wife, Margaret, and their children lived in a large house outside the City. Joseph went home to his family on the weekends.

Joseph's wife, Margaret, stayed home with the children. Since she was rich, she had servants to help with the housework and nurses to help care for the children. She had time to read a lot. And she kept a diary. After she died, her diary was published as a good example to other women of how to live.

Joseph Woods liked to read, too. He read all the latest books. He knew so much about books that people in America asked for his help. Benjamin Franklin had started a library in Philadelphia, Pennsylvania. Franklin and his friends wanted to read all the latest books, too. But it was hard to get books. They asked Joseph Woods to get books in London and send them across the ocean. Woods sent many books to the library in Philadelphia. Do you have a library near you? Do you like to go there to read?

Joseph Woods read a lot about trade. One kind of trade that had been going on for a long time was the slave trade. British slave traders would go to Africa and capture natives there. Then, the slave traders would take the Africans to islands or to lands in America and sell them.

Joseph Woods made his living by trade, but he did not think the slave trade was right. Joseph said Africans were human beings, and buying and selling human beings was not right. He said people in Britain should outlaw the slave trade. At first, not many people agreed with Joseph Woods and his friends. But in 1807, the British government outlawed the slave trade.

While Joseph Woods was writing about the slave trade, other people were writing about the rights of men and the rights of women. Joseph Woods made fun of ideas about the rights of women. Margaret Woods "knew not what to think." But Margaret did think women should "look upon men as superiors." Although Joseph Woods did not believe the slave trade was right, he and Margaret did not believe in equal rights for everyone. Do you understand their point of view?

Made in the U.S.A.

In 1776, some people in North America began fighting against the British. Before the fighting began, Joseph Woods thought the British were too hard on the Americans. He thought people in America should have the same rights as people in Britain. After the fighting started, Joseph Woods supported the British side.

The British lost the war, and some of the lands they had ruled became the United States of America. But people still came to the United States from all parts of Britain. People came here from England, Wales, Scotland, and Ireland. Some of these people had last names that related to work, like Shepherd, Carpenter, Weaver, and Smith. People came to the United States from other countries, too, like Sweden, Germany, and France. Did any of your relatives come here from any of those countries?

Why do you think so many people came to the United States to live? People probably came here for lots of different reasons. Many came to find a better way of life, to make more money, and to have more rights. Some came to get land. Land was an important way to get money, status, and a better life.

After the United States became independent,

people began moving west to get more land. But Native Americans were using the lands in the West. Native Americans had different ideas about working and about owning land. But because most Native Americans could not read or write, they had a hard time getting their ideas across. So fighting broke out again. And the natives lost again.

While some people in Britain were coming to the United States to get land, others were inventing new machines to make things to trade. First came machines to make cotton cloth faster and cheaper than men and women could make it by hand. Then came machines to make steam for railroads and boats.

When people came to the United States from Britain and other places, they brought new machines or ideas for new machines with them. People in the United States seemed to like machines. They used machines and ideas from other places and thought up new machines and ideas of their own.

In the 1800s, some men made lots of money with new machines and new ideas. Henry Ford figured out how to make cars faster and cheaper. John D. Rockefeller found new ways of getting and selling oil. Andrew Carnegie made stronger steel. Cornelius Vanderbilt built many railroads.

Today, people have figured out how to use

machines for just about everything. Think about how we get food now. For most people, hunting for meat means going to the grocery store. We have machines for tilling, plowing, reaping, and picking fruits and vegetables. Food is frozen, packaged, and canned.

Susan Sexton from Pike County, Kentucky, worked in a corn canning factory. She worked from 6:00 p.m. to 6:00 a.m., and she "picked bad corn from good corn." She sat "on a chair like a stool with a belt running in front" of her and a pole beside her "with a little bucket on the pole." She wrote, "If I found a worm or a bug, I would put it in the bucket. Sometimes before the night was over, I would fall asleep for a little while. The noise from the factory would awake me." That's a lot different from the way prehistoric people got corn to eat.

Machines have changed reading and writing. Remember Christine de Pisan? She wrote each of her books by hand. If she wanted another copy, she copied it over by hand. Today, we have typewriters, computers, printing presses, and copying machines. We don't just write now, we communicate. So we have telegrams, telephones, and television to help us communicate faster without our having to write a word.

Machines have changed how we get from one

place to another. Christopher Columbus crossed the ocean in a sailboat. Today, we can cross the ocean by steamboat, nuclear submarine, or jet plane. On land, we have cars, coaches, trains, and buses. Spaceships can take us to the moon and beyond. Do you think Hesiod would consider space travel risky?

Machines have changed the way we get food. Machines have changed how and what we trade. Machines have changed what we see, hear, and read. Machines have changed our lives and continue to change them today. What do you think about these changes?

I've Been Working on the Railroad

Machines have changed the way we work. They have also changed some of our sayings, songs, and ideas about work. We have a lot of old sayings about work. Have you ever heard people say they had "a hard row to hoe"? Or has anyone told you to "make hay while the sun shines"? Do you know what a "spinster" is? Can you guess what kind of work a spinster did?

Another old saying is "A man may work from sun to sun, but a woman's work is never done." Have you ever heard that saying? Do you think it holds true today? Do you think your answer to that question might depend on your point of view?

In the late 1800s and early 1900s, new kinds of work brought in new kinds of songs and sayings. Take railroads, for example. A hundred or so years ago, lots of people were working hard to build railroads all over the United States. Have you ever heard the song "I've Been Working on the Railroad"?

Coal mining is another example. Coal mining is hard work, even with machines. Do you remember "Sixteen Tons," sung by Tennessee Ernie Ford? In the song, he says he loaded sixteen tons of number nine coal. And all he got was another day older and deeper in debt. But Loretta Lynn, a singer from Kentucky, is proud to be "A Coal Miner's Daughter."

Machines have changed the way women and men work, but machines have not changed all of our old ideas about work. Some people say it is bad luck for a woman to go into an underground mine. Other people say it is bad luck for men to stir gravy. Do you think some kinds of work are more suited for women than men? Do you think some kinds of work are more suited for men than women? Do you think a man and a woman might have different points of view about what is woman's work and what is man's work?

Machines are also changing our ideas about learning to read. For a long time, people could get work without knowing how to read. And some people still can. Aggie Fink, who lives in Meta, Kentucky, did not learn to read when she was younger, but she did learn a trade.

Aggie says, "What I, Aggie Fink, do for a living is something you read about earlier, prehistoric people sewing skins and furs together to make their clothes. I am a seamstress, a craft that has been handed down from generation to generation in my family—my mother taught me, and her mother taught her. I see this as a gift of God."

But machines have made it harder for some people to find work, especially if they can't read. Bruce, another student in the new readers' program, did not learn to read when he was young. But, unlike Aggie, Bruce did not learn a trade or craft. Bruce "got into drugs and drinking" and had trouble finding work.

Bruce says, "I worked mostly at hard labor jobs. I worked for a carpenter and had to carry the wood. People considered me a work mule. I got tired of this job and found another one even harder, digging in the dirt. I guess this was the hardest job I ever had."

What about you? What kind of work have you done? Do you know any songs or sayings about work? Do you work with machines? Is learning how to read changing the way you work or do other things?

Work and Play

You have been reading a lot about work. Has reading so much about work made you tired? Let's call time out on work. Let's take a break. Let's think about *play*.

What is *play*, anyway? Some people might say play is the opposite of work. If work is something you do to make money or to earn a living, does that mean *play* is something you do for free? But what about someone who *plays* golf or tennis for a living? Or what about people who make money (or lose money) by *playing* cards, *playing* the horses, or *playing* the lottery? Some people *play* for keeps.

While some people *play* games, other people *play* music. Some women and men and even little children can *play* the piano or the banjo. Others can only *play* the radio. Some *play* music for fun, but some *play* for money. Could it be that *play* is something we do because we want to—whether or not we get paid for it?

Playing is something we do, but a *play* can be a work of art. A person can write a *play*, or drama. Then, actors act out the *play* for others to see. In a *play*, actors *play* the parts of real people. When you were little, did you ever *play* like you were someone else? Even though we haven't all been in a *play*, most of us have *played* the fool at one time or another.

So play is not as simple as it might seem. Like work, play means different things to different people. And, like work, play has been an important part of human history from the beginning. Play was around even before written history. Do you remember what the time before written history is called?

According to experts, people in prehistoric times probably didn't work as many hours as we do today. Prehistoric people hunted when they needed food. They tended the fields when the plants needed tending. There were children to care for and other kinds of work. But there were no houses to clean, cars to wash, or yards to mow.

So prehistoric people had time to sing songs, tell stories, and eat big meals (that is, when plenty of food was available). Prehistoric people in the northwestern part of the United States, for example, could catch all the fish they needed in six months. Then, they could take it easy for the rest of the year!

During the time of Hesiod, Greeks played by competing at sports. About the time Hesiod was writing poems, others were keeping records of special games held every four years at a place called Olympia. These games became known as the Olympics. The main event of the Olympics was a short race called the *stade*. Today, a place where sports events are held is called a stadium. The stadium at Olympia seated 40 thousand people.

The Greeks had other kinds of games and matches. Most sports were for men, but one race was for 16 unmarried women. There were also contests to see who could play the best music or write the best poems. Hesiod was very proud to have won a poetry contest. The Greeks also wrote plays for special events. Plays and playing were an important part of life for the Greeks. The Greeks liked to compete. Do you?

Plays were also important during the time of Christine de Pisan. The Roman Catholic church was very important in Italy, France, and other places in the Middle Ages. Plays written in the Middle Ages were usually about religion. A play often told a story from the Bible.

People in the Middle Ages also told stories and sang songs. The stories and songs that weren't about religion were about love and romance. Romance was big in the Middle Ages. Do you think romance is big in stories and songs today?

Because the Catholic church was so important in the Middle Ages, people celebrated holy days. On these days, they did not work. Saint Valentine's Day was in February, for example. Lady Day, in honor of the Virgin Mary, was on March 25. People gave each other eggs on Easter. Christmas lasted for 12 days to mark the time from the birth of the baby until the coming of the Wise Men. Saint Nicholas brought gifts during those 12 days.

Holidays were also important to Joseph and Margaret Woods in the 1700s, but not for religious reasons. Just about every summer, Joseph and Margaret Woods took their children on holiday to a seaside resort. They rented a house, complete with dishes and linens, near the sea. Margaret and Joseph and their children took long walks and ate picnics. If they wanted to swim, they got into a bathing machine. A bathing machine was something like a booth on wheels without a floor. Margaret told how she got into a machine and rolled into the water so she could swim without being seen by anyone!

During the rest of the year, Joseph Woods relaxed by going to coffeehouses and talking to his friends. He read the newspapers and heard the latest news. He had time to read and think about trade. Margaret Woods stayed at home, except for the family holidays. She read, wrote letters, and kept her journal. Since she had servants to help with the housework, she had time for her reading and writing. Do you like to spend your free time reading or writing?

What is work and what is play depend a lot on your point of view. Aggie Fink, from Meta, in Pike County, Kentucky, has her own ideas about work and play. "Most people say that what you do for a living is your work; not always!" Aggie wrote. "Real work is doing something that is hard for you. You have to stick with work to get it done. Something that is not a gift to you would be work, as reading is to me. Spelling is the hardest work I do!"

Working in the World Today

Now you know how all sorts of folks in different times and places worked and played. What about work today? Is work today a lot like it was in the past, or is work today very different?

The world is a big place, and all kinds of people do all kinds of different work. In some places, like Africa and South America, many people still farm much as prehistoric people did. Look back at the map on page 18. Find Africa and South America. Many people there today don't have much cash money and have to work hard just to stay alive.

Even in our own country, there are many different kinds of work today. Not too many people in the United States make their living by farming any more. Most people live in cities. Kentucky is one state where many people still live in the country. Do you live in the city or in the country? Which do you like best, the city or the country?

After machines like trains and cars were invented, more and more people in the United States left the country to live in the city. In Kentucky, many people moved to Louisville and Lexington to find work. Other people from Kentucky moved to Cincinnati,

Ohio, or Chicago, Illinois, or Detroit, Michigan, to find work. One of my uncles moved from Kentucky to Detroit to work in a car factory. Another uncle moved from Kentucky to Columbus, Ohio, to get a job as a meat packer. Have you or any of your relatives ever moved to a city to find work?

Like Joseph Woods a long time ago, many folks who work in the city today still want to be in the country. Some people have country houses or take vacations in the country. Other people work in the city but have homes in the country. These people sometimes drive many miles for an hour or more to get from home to work. People who don't have cars or can't drive might have a hard time getting work today. What about you?

How people work in other countries makes a difference to us in the United States. Workers in Japan, for example, make cars a lot like cars in the United States. Some people here think cars made in Japan are better or cheaper, so they buy Japanese cars. Workers in Australia mine coal and sell it to the Japanese. American companies also mine coal to sell to Japan. Does that mean the workers or the companies are competing with each other?

Which do you think is more important, the kind of work a person does or where he or she lives? Do you think a car worker in the United States would be very much like a car worker in Japan or completely different? What do you think it would be like to live and work in a different country in the world today? Would you like to try?

Working in the World Tomorrow

What do you think work will be like in the future? Can you imagine what life will be like in the years to come? What do you think will be happening 50 years from today? What about 100 years from now?

Like the big machines of the past, computers could change the work of the future. Computers are already writing letters, doing math, drawing charts, keeping records, and talking on the phone. Many people like to play computer games. Computers are already changing the way we work and the way we play.

Since most computers work by numbers and letters, it helps to know how to read to use a computer. But computers can also help people learn to read. Do you know how to use a computer? Do you want to know how to use a computer? In the future what do you think will happen to people who can't read if more and more work is done by computers?

No matter what their size or strength, people can use computers. Even little children use computers for work and play. You can use a computer at home as well as in an office. Do you think that means more people will be working at home in the future? If that happens, will housework still be something that women do at home? Could computers make it easier for single mothers, like Christine de Pisan, to stay home and earn a living? Would men and women be paid equally for doing the same type of work at home on a computer?

People are already working fewer hours because of computers and other machines. Do you think people will only work two or three days a week in the future? If that happens, what will folks do with their time? Will people spend more time outside, hunting, fishing, playing sports, and in their gardens? Or will they stay inside reading, watching television, and playing computer games?

Computers are already changing the music we hear and what we see on television. Do you think computers will change our minds or our ideas? Will we have songs like "I've Been Working on the Computer?" Or, how about "I Loaded 16 Bytes of Elite Type"? Or, maybe, "I'm Proud to be a Computer Programmer's Daughter"? Do you think computers could change our ideas about what is men's work and what is women's work? What do you think work will be like in the world tomorrow?

Why Work?

You have been working hard at learning more about work. But this work is about to come to an end. You have read about *how* people worked in times past. But we haven't really thought much about *why*. Why do you think people work?

Prehistoric people worked to get the food and things they needed to stay alive. Hesiod worked to get ahead and be as rich as his neighbor. Christine de Pisan worked to support her family. Joseph Woods worked to be able to live in a certain style. Do you think these same reasons apply today? Can you think of other reasons for working?

As you know, work has changed a lot since early times. We no longer grow food or make books or sell wool the way people did back then. But some of our *ideas* about work haven't changed much. Hesiod thought everyone should work. He said that not working was a "disgrace." Christine de Pisan was most concerned with status and paid more attention to the work of high-ranking women. Joseph Woods thought the slave trade was wrong, but he did not think Africans or women were his equals.

Maybe we need to think again about some of our

old ideas about work. With all our new machines, experts say people will work fewer hours in the future. Will not working still be a disgrace then? What about people who are retired or disabled? And what about people who want to work but can't find jobs?

And what about status? In Hesiod's day, a farmer had very high status. Do you think farmers still have high status today? Why or why not? What kind of work has high status today? What kind of work does not have status? Do you think different workers would have different answers to these questions?

And what about rights? Joseph Woods believed that freedom was a basic right for all human beings. But he did not believe in equal rights for everyone. Do you think that everyone *should* have equal rights today? Do you think everyone *does* have equal rights?

Work is not always easy, even today with all our machines. And it's not always easy to find work. There sure aren't any easy answers to some of these questions about work. It looks like we'll just have to keep on working on some of our ideas about work.

About the Author

Judi Jennings was born in Lexington, Kentucky, and received her B.A. from the University of Kentucky. With little thought of future employment, she pursued a graduate degree in eighteenth-century British history. She studied at the Institute of Historical Research in London in 1973 before receiving her Ph.D. at the University of Kentucky in 1975. While teaching at Union College in Barbourville, she developed a love of Eastern Kentucky. Another year in London in 1982 convinced her there's no place like home. Returning to Central Kentucky, she worked at the Kentucky Department for Libraries and Archives and the Kentucky Humanities Council. Since 1987 she has worked at Appalshop in Whitesburg because she believes it is important for the people of Eastern Kentucky to have opportunities to speak for themselves and to try solving their own problems, and that is what Appalshop is about.